D1482363

art

as the measure of man
by george d. stoddard

as education
by irwin edman

a personal vision
by bruno bettelheim

the museum of
modern art, new york

published for the
national committee on
art education

distributed by
doubleday & co., inc.
garden city, n.y.

© 1964, The Museum of Modern Art
11 West 53 Street, New York 19, N. Y.

Library of Congress Catalogue Card No. 64-15286
Printed in the U.S.A. by Plantin Press, New York
Designed by Werner Brudi

The three lectures published in this book were major addresses at three different Annual Conferences of the National Committee on Art Education. **Art as a Measure of Man,** by George D. Stoddard, Chancellor of New York University, was given in 1963; **Art: A Personal Vision,** by Bruno Bettelheim, Professor of Psychology, University of Chicago, in 1962; and **Art as Education,** by the late Irwin Edman, Professor of Philosophy, Columbia University, in 1950.

The word "art" is common to the three titles and is the focus of the lectures, but they are not discourses on art as an aesthetic doctrine, a technique or a style. Art is conceived in its broadest philosophical sense, as man's spiritual language or as Alfred H. Barr, Jr. once called it, "a visual esperanto," and as a way of ennobling life.

While methods and techniques of education may change, the philosophical and spiritual role of art remains constant and fundamental, if one conceives of art education as the means of developing the creative spirit of man. The essence of each lecture is summed up in the following quotations:

But the paradox is that, stripped of all pretenses, art retains its power as the most original and delightful of all human endeavors that get beyond the acts and events of the day. It survives all its phases. It has no place to go except forward. Man himself can do no better.—George D. Stoddard

The constricted life of our educational system conceals from students the vast light and mysteries of the world they inhabit. May art education withdraw these blinders from the eyes of students so that through your teaching they will behold the great light of their innermost world.—Bruno Bettelheim

No reflection on anything these days can responsibly be made without consideration of its consequences for the perils and contingencies of democratic civilization in the western world. The creation of art is the self-discipline of free minds. Its order is that of individuals at once vital and self-harmonized. In art are instances, more winning than argument, of what free society may achieve.—Irwin Edman

Someone has wisely said, "art education is everybody's business," which means, I believe, that if art is to give its full measure of value, everyone—the parent, the administrator, the business man, the man in the street—must understand and support its contribution to the individual and to the total society. This book, then, is not only for the art teacher, the educator or the specialist. It is for everyone. Though the book is small, the authors speak of art and education in their largest dimensions. They are timely and timeless.

VICTOR D'AMICO
Executive Director, National Committee on Art Education

CONTENTS

Art as the Measure of Man
george d. stoddard
new york university

The aim of education is life fulfillment through learn-ing and the creative process. Education is ongoing. We may judge its effectiveness by its results but its results are more than objects; they are conceptual. Under the right conditions, this process of insight-into-action leads to a work of art. If this is to happen, one necessary ingredient is **talent** and another is **skill,** but the truly rare factor is **intellect.** Through it all, we perceive a high degree of intensity and perseverance —of dedication, if you will. The artist or any other creative person produces something. He thinks things through, albeit speedily and with emotion. And then he works things through, for if he does not, he re-mains a dreamer, an escapist, a dilettante.

Every creative effort and every end-product is, like each individual person, unique. After a time, not even identical twins are alike; each one weaves into his personality and experience something new and dif-ferent. So it is with true artists under the same teacher, the same ground rules, and the same cul-tural conditions—the sameness is superficial. If the artist fails to get away from his teacher or his school, he is forever imitative and inferior; if his view of the world does not contain something peculiar to him, he might better take up bookkeeping or bricklaying.

Of course with students, we need not fear; variety is the sign of life. The work may be creative and pleasant, but it takes enormous discipline to develop something that is not only original but also good. And to be good in any educational or artistic endeavor means to evoke thought and emotion in others. Thus the actor must express emotions in ways that communicate more than the real experience; his whisper of dismay must be heard and reacted to a long way off. Thus the writer has to get inside the minds of his characters—whether they be dogs, apes or men—and he must be allowed to roam at will, in utter defiance of space, time or common sense. Similarly the graphic artist keeps trying to penetrate all his worlds, possible or impossible, replacing conventional abstractions by wilder ones. Perhaps, if we become too familiar with the work of the "abstractionists" in form and color, they will turn back to stir us with more traditional abstractions.

In any case we should not lose sight of the fact that all art is based on illusion, abstraction, and the exercise of intelligence. Not long ago, speaking of creativity in education, I said (from H. H. Anderson, ed., **Creativity and Its Cultivation,** Harper, N. Y., 1959):

We should not overemphasize the technique of vision. We cannot think with the eyes, and we may think without them. Vision brings in the data, the raw materials, and the cues that guide our steps. The eye is an invaluable sense organ, a true part of the brain through its optic nerve, but the frontal lobes preside over the problems created and they are not to be denied. The artist is a man seeing and thinking—both at once; his cunning is in his brain. It is not enough for him to experience beauty or love or hate; he must get it down on something at least two-dimensional. The artist is uncommon because speech is common. If man had kept to visual patterns and had not developed speech except in a gifted few, speech might have become the main vehicle of artistic endeavor. If everybody talked by drawing, and only a few by speaking, we would regard every manifestation of speech as a work of art—good, bad, or unintelligible. In fact, primitive Norsemen did regard writing as a form of magic and therefore, reprehensible. Talking has made babblers of us all, so that only the low idiots lack the gift to some degree. For us the difference between speech and graphic art is that in art few try. The painting, unless it carries the impact of a blinker sign, is regarded as tough reading with no reader's guide. (pp. 193-94)

The artist seeks the meaning that is lost in the casual. If he achieves it for himself, he still cannot achieve it for us, but only offers us a better basis for finding the meaning than we might otherwise discover. He works hard at the task. He extracts, selects, arranges, does what we have little time or talent to do. Admittedly, if he fails to communicate, the failure may be in us. It is wrong to hold, however, that the failure is always in us—the observers—for to do so would make painting as empty as a crystal ball. The archaic picture on the cave wall meant something that needed no reference to words to make it a passion to its creator fresh from the hunt. He saw; he felt. He transmitted, sometimes with wonderfully accurate drawing, the essence of the experience. Such works, devoid of borrowing from a culture pattern, are close to the heart of creativity. (p. 194)

Since art portrays ideas, the student's approach to it must be intellectual. If he creates something, the thing may be only two-dimensional—as in photography or a play of light to form designs and colors—or essentially two-dimensional as in drawing or paint-

ing. In the plastic arts, architecture and the performing arts we utilize three dimensions, but they, too,
may be reducible to two dimensions as subject matter for drawings and paintings. But the creative concept itself is as nondimensional as thought, for the
very good reason that **it is thought.** The concept
itself is not a work of art; it has to be represented in
a form communicable to others, that is, as designs,
words or actions.

It follows that no measure of artistic merit can be
directly derived from its adherence to realism, natu-
ralism, impressionism, abstractionism or the like;
they all embody **abstract ideas.** If some forms are
imitative of real objects—let us say, prosaic photographs of prosaic objects, the photographs are
nonetheless abstract. If a garbage heap is reduced
to the size of a postage stamp, what is **real** about the
representation? Since such a photograph probably
is not art, the criteria of what is aesthetically good
and what is cheap or bad must be found elsewhere.

Art is indeed a language, a form of communication, but if we are to bring it home to the classroom,
the studio or the exhibit, we must differentiate it
from other mental activities. John Dewey, looking at
the question as a psychologist and philosopher, said
thirty years ago (John Dewey, **Art As Experience,**
G. P. Putnam's & Sons, New York, 1934, 1958):

Expression strikes below the barriers that separate
human beings from one another. Since art is the most
universal form of language, since it is constituted, even
apart from literature, by the common qualities of the public world, it is the most universal and freest form of com-

munication. Every intense experience of friendship and affection completes itself artistically. The sense of communion generated by a work of art may take on a definitely religious quality. The union of men with one another is the source of the rites that from the time of archaic man to the present have commemorated the crises of birth, death and marriage. Art is the extension of the power of rites and ceremonies to unite men, through a shared celebration, to all incidents and scenes of life. This office is the reward and seal of art. That art weds man and nature is a familiar fact. Art also renders men aware of their union with one another in origin and destiny. (pp. 270-71)

Rite and ceremony as well as legend bound the living and the dead in a common partnership. They were esthetic but they were more than esthetic. The rites of mourning expressed more than grief; the war and harvest dance were more than a gathering of energy for tasks to be performed; magic was more than a way of commanding forces of nature to do the bidding of man; feasts were more than a satisfaction of hunger. Each of these communal modes of activity united the practical, the social and the educative in an integrated whole having esthetic form. They introduced social values into experience in a way that was most impressive. They connected things that were overtly important and overtly done with the substantial life of the community. Art was **in** them, for these activities conformed to the needs and conditions of the most intense, most readily grasped and longest remembered experience. (pp. 327-28)

Such a view is scarcely consistent with an artificial imposition of art training from above or from without. If the student cannot escape his environment, he can, at least, be encouraged to get his sense of direction from within. Along this line Conant and Randall (Howard Conant and Arne Randall, **Art**

in Education, Chas. A. Bennett, Peoria, Ill., 1959)
quote Victor d'Amico as follows:

The great value of creative experience is that it pro-
vides for and develops personal integration, because the
child selects his own motivation and expresses himself
in terms of his own needs and aptitudes. The sensitive
art teacher guides the child into experience most suited
to his ability and most satisfying to his individual concepts, at a rate of learning natural to him. The curriculum
approach is apt to destroy personal integration because
the motivation comes from subject matter, such as social
studies or science, allowing little expression for emotional needs or creative concepts. (p. 290)

They also quote Viktor Lowenfeld, as follows:

Teachers often think if history is illustrated, or inter-
preted in the art lesson, integration of two subject matters takes place. This is by no means true. In such a
superficial situation, neither history is explained, nor
does a creative experience become meaningful. . . . Integration does not occur from the outside; integration
is not 'made' by 'assembling' two subjects; integration
happens from within. That says clearly that integration
can only take place by self-indentification. The integrated
art experiences of the settlers who landed on our shores
will, therefore, be different for each individual, accord-
ing to the type of self-identification which takes place in
each individual. (pp. 291-92)

Since a student will appreciate a work of art in
terms of its power to evoke in him some new response, it is a task of the teacher to aid in this process. Perhaps that is why many works of art carry a
name or title. They carry it as a symbolic reference to
something the artist and the viewer intellectually
share in another context. Untitled, or with the title
withheld, there has to be some element that permits

communication. Thus Michelangelo's **David** carries a special connotation that means little to modern youth. Untitled but displayed as a nude, handsome young man it would doubtless be equally admired. Similarly for the ancient gods and goddesses whose names and addresses are lost upon the present generation of students. Today, a place name, a classical or Biblical reference, may or may not enhance the appeal; it may lead only to puzzlement. Of the tens of thousands of persons who recently viewed Rembrandt's **Aristotle Contemplating a Bust of Homer,** how many knew anything about the poet, the philosopher, or, for that matter, the painter? **Mona Lisa** smiles as a woman, whether in Italy, France or the United States; it leads few persons to restudy the Renaissance. Cézanne's "Uncle" is anybody's hard-bitten relative.

In these examples we get an intensive communication that could be enhanced by history and biography. For the teacher and the student we could get much more. We could show what has to be the nature of the talent, the technique, the striving—often the anguish—to produce such lasting effects. Never again should the informed student underplay either the achievement or the significance of great art in any form in any age. He will measure the distance between himself and the master; once in a million times, it may not be too great. The good teacher knows this and he has something for each student— an example in art beyond one's capacity to equal it, but quite within the range of enjoyment and inspi-

ration of countless students and adults who will take
the trouble to observe, to compare, to understand.
So it is with music, drama and literature.

Howard Conant goes so far as to place this experience at the core of art education. He says **(Art
Education Bulletin,** May, 1960):

The primary function of art education is to develop
consumer taste—a working knowledge of art—in people
of all ages who are now suffering from acute aesthetic
anemia. There must be vastly increased attention to the
aesthetic needs of boys and girls in elementary and sec-
ondary schools. Beginning in the primary grade, children
should develop familiarity with important examples of the
arts. **The finest, most natural, and clearly the most effective way to do this is to place important, original painting, sculpture and craft objects in school classrooms and
corridors.** (p. 8)

Conant's reference is to all art forms—graphic
and plastic works, craft objects, textiles and indus-
trial designs. The masters can be represented by
first-rate reproductions. Such works are not to be
glimpsed, but studied and understood—woven into
one's visual, intellectual and emotional experience.

Some educational misconceptions may arise from
a failure to realize that art is nonscientific. Its so-
called formulas are inexact; they are not stated as
equations, problems, or laws. Also art is nonstatisti-
cal; what counts is the individual artist and a particular product. Nonobjective art is not an abstraction in
any algebraic or geometric sense. In science to express in symbols or drawings is inevitably **only** to
illustrate. Except in the mind's eye there is no such
thing as a triangle; it has shape and nothing but

shape—no size, no color, no texture, no implicit significance. Likewise the uniquely valuable concept of zero in mathematics has no counterpart in art; it does not imply negation or emptiness, and certainly not a reduction to absurdity.

The ancient Greeks had need of science and technology in a world dominated by the arts and philosophy. Aristotle showed the way, but for two thousand years he was not followed. We cannot now go back to prescientific days, but the plain truth is not that science will fail to advance but that henceforth the human race may have relatively small need of such advances. True, there are a few diseases yet to be conquered, but they are outnumbered, a hundred to one, by medical services we now know how to render, but do not. Ill health, disease and death are concomitants of practices known without any further technical advances to be faulty but deeply ingrained in personal choice and the social structure. In the midst of an extraordinary sophistication in the application of science we remain fearful and frustrated in the realms of personality, politics and social welfare.

What has this to do with art? Well, if art is to be taken as a measure of man, we need a better understanding of the human being and the human condition. We cannot truthfully assert, as a perverse religious sentiment, that all is disease and disrepair, but we can say with conviction that the whole world may be moving fast toward a total destruction, not only of the amenities of life, but of life itself.

Except through art, no man is immortal. History records; it enlarges and embellishes its subject matter of men and events. History plays up and it plays down, but the end result is diminution and dismissal unless art intervenes. Every conquest, to survive and remain meaningful, must be measured in the quality of the art it engenders, whether the times be those of the Egyptians, the Assyrians, the Greeks or the Romans, or the fifteen centuries since. Every dogma, discovery or political reform, in fact, every scientific advance gets accounted for in terms of its meaning, and its meaning inevitably finds expression in the literary, visual and performing arts. But that is not the whole range of art in civilization. While it is unlikely that art **precedes** the event, the insight or the achievement, it certainly does accompany aspiration and pave the way to new advances. The heroes and saints of one age, through art, are able to inspire new generations.

It follows that to respond intelligently to the power of art to arouse us is to achieve a new dimension in the understanding of history, religion and social structure. The only way we can transcend the dying person which is every man is to make of him, and of all like him, a myth, and this is done invariably through art. The historical existence or character of the person is, in fact, irrelevant. Of the past, we know only the art-created man. If, like Zeus, or Mars, or Hamlet, or Mephistopheles, he did not exist at all, it matters little. Masters in the arts of language, visual form and movement will create and maintain him in our thoughts and dreams like one of us.

The arts of man may well outlive the human race

that produced them, yielding a future on this earth somewhat like its archaic past—a world without land animals. But with a difference! Some inanimate products of man's short period of natural dominance will survive the effects of fire, blast and poison. Uncomprehending vegetation will grow in the shadow of the pyramids, the great dams and the enduring rubble of cities. Fish may crawl out of the sea on their stubby, finny legs to start again the endless cycle. After all, even the fish will know as much about their new environment and its left-over fragments as man himself knew about his environment only 100,000 years ago. And we know so little now! Only enough to sense our weakness, our impotence, our utter insignificance on any scale of cosmic events. Only enough to realize that if life is to be worth living, it must be so in terms of a constant search for truth, beauty and humanity, each attribute affected by the other and no one, taken alone, sufficient for the peace of mind of modern man.

Art is a form of truth, and truth of many sorts is revealed in and through art. Thus, if I may be more practical, science, with its handmaiden, technology, is essential as a shield against hunger, disease, slavery and superstition, and as a structural form for social progress. Art, on the other hand, is essential if we are to keep above the other animals and in control of the animal drives within us. Art is a measure of what we most want to record, to preserve, to hand down in an alternating current of humility and pride. I have indicated that art involves an illusion, namely, that the transformation of what the sense organs bring us and the brain electrically integrates is a greater reality than any immediate psychological sensation. We seek and cling to the personification. We are so constructed physically, so conditioned psychologically and so organized socially as to be compelled to interweave fact and fancy, object and dream-object, experience and hope. We can no more go back to atomistic responses than the body itself can to its chemical and physical ingredients.

In the triad referred to above, humanity—a term signifying love and brotherhood and justice—seems to hold the highest place. This makes sense to me, but it should not be construed to mean that science and art are subservient in any vulgar way. Quite the reverse! Science stands on its own feet; it needs no help at all from art. In fact, if art teachers stretch themselves in order to aid science, the result may be useless to the scientist and humiliating to the artist. The engine, the dynamo and the airplane may be beautiful objects, but that, if I may say so, is not their object; they represent neither science nor art, as such. Of course, scientific formulations and discoveries lie back of each design, but science stopped there—stopped with the problem, the process, the solution. Dressed-up, the machine becomes a ship, a plane, an automobile, and now there is scope for the object to become not only an end-point in the application of scientific principles but a starting point for creative artistic ventures. The ship as a three-dimensional functioning object may be intrinsically beautiful; it may meet the criteria of a work of art. On the other hand, it may be functional and at the same time ugly—by its nature, or perhaps by the indifference of its designer. It is simply an accident that some mechanical forms strike us as beautiful; we like to think of beauty as an attribute of function. In the object or life form itself, this does not follow. The solar-powered space vehicle with its great wing flaps is an ugly thing and so is the hyena or the balloon fish. Who is to say that the space contraption is less efficient than the graceful jet liner or the knobby swelling fish inferior to the trout? I suppose the Australian jackrabbit is not as graceful, and therefore not as beautiful, as the common American deer. Nature and science, after all, may get results in ways not aesthetically pleasing to the human taste. When the world of nature does manifest itself in beautiful shapes, colors and movements, there is no doubt that the botanist, the marine biologist and the astronomer are delighted by the convergence.

It is easy to be misunderstood at this point. Ugliness anywhere may become a thing of beauty, or in any event something to hold us and lift us up, through the magic touch of the artist in any medium. In a harsh and bitter world we cannot shut our eyes to disappointment and danger. Does not all great art, however beautiful its forms, reveal the ephemeral nature of the individual or the tendency to self-destruction of the human race? In all history are there any examples of courage, nobility and self-sacrifice without the counterpart forces of cowardice, cruelty and lust for power? Art may reveal all sides of every question, but not as a means of resolving the issues. It can help us to remember, to understand, to take action, but it will do so only by clinging to its own standards and its unique freedom. Political art, poster art, "cheesecake" art are self-defeating, as art forms, however successful they may be otherwise. They are likely to proclaim an untruth as truth, a tyrant as a friend of the people and ugly social situations as a gift from heaven.

As we place humanity at the top of the social structure, the paradox is that we allot to both science and art the wonderful twin gifts of freedom and responsibility, confident that only by so doing can we preserve the highest values of the whole man.

As an outsider looking in, I have been especially intrigued by some statements of Peter Fingesten. He writes (**The Art Journal,** Fall, 1961, XXI, 1):

We know that Kandinsky and Mondrian derived their theoretical background from Theosophy; mandalas may have given them certain formal elements. Since Mondrian indicated in his early notebooks that he believed in meditation practices, it is more than likely that he was familiar with these mystic diagrams of oriental religions. A mandala is a magic circle or square (or a square within a circle) drawn on paper or on the ground, or made of butter, rice and other materials. It is an abstract pattern upon which the devotee, monk or yogin meditates, for the center of the mandala is believed to be the seat of a deity. During meditation these mandalas become charged with immense power and the deity appears before the mental eye of the devotee. He identifies with it and often imagines that he himself is the god to whose perfection he aspires. Mandalas are also used in magic by lamas to acquire superhuman powers, or **siddhis.** Such mandalas have been used in the East since time immemorial and are evidence of the oriental antecedence of the theory that abstract patterns are charged with energy or spiritual forces. Certain remarks by Kandinsky confirm his belief in the latent spiritual powers of geometric designs. . . . The severe grid system of Mondrian's style profoundly affected international achitecture, interior decoration, commercial art, typography and other fields of creative endeavor. Kandinsky, on the other hand, freed the artist's subconscious and substantially altered the history of painting towards a direct translation of the artist's intuition of the inner forces of nature. We are today surrounded by symbols of the equivalence of spirit and matter. But this is exactly what was desired by these artists for whom art was an implement in the evolution of man towards a greater awareness of the world of the spirit. . . . The founders of the non-objective styles of art either identified with mystical movements or thought in terms of extreme subjective realism, aesthetically as well as philosophically. . . . Zen Buddhism has the same significance for the younger American abstract expressionists that Theosophy had for the founders. (p. 4)

Being neither artist nor art critic, but only a former psychologist, I cannot vouch for the accuracy or authority of this statement. Still, since it appeared in a recent issue of **The Art Journal,** let us assume that it represents a substantial body of opinion in the world of art.

We must admit that most men are no longer moved by the dry-bones rattling of theology. Western peoples, except as a kind of sentimental fringe benefit, do not expect to purify their souls by renouncing the world. Frequently, they do all too good a job of escaping from reality, but they wind up not in retreats or sacred resorts, but in sick wards and sanitariums.

For us, it follows that if Kandinsky and his followers were Theosophists and painted accordingly, their inspiration, like their style, is an oriental importation of limited significance in Western cultures. Devoid of even these esoteric roots, the imitators of such a style would be expected to deteriorate. I do not, of course, refer to nonsymbolic designs that give us pleasure and serve to enliven the arts of decoration. I refer only to the futile attempts of observers either to read meaning into symbols of which they are ignorant or to impose symbols upon a nonsymbolic treatment of subject matter.

Of such painting, Fingesten says:

No verbal gymnastics will make its mysteries more comprehensible precisely because one symbolism cannot be substituted for another. (p. 6)

And again, he says:

Non-objective art has broken through the process of symbolization itself . . . (its) formal referents are not symbols in the traditional sense, evoking something outside of themselves, but . . . simply are without denotative content altogether. (p. 5)

What does it all come down to? Let us assume the founders of nonobjective art were deeply moved by symbols which for them, as for millions of oriental devotees, carried the deepest significance. In this respect their work is akin to the great mass of art from antiquity to our day, for that, too, has been based on religious myths, rites and symbolic figures. The enduring works of art, pagan or Judaeo-Christian, certainly carried a powerful message. They denoted persons and events that were infinitely precious, and they were capable of evoking the full range of human emotions. By such symbols, aesthetic or not, men lived and died, or perhaps concentrated on the destruction of others. For East and West those days are indeed over. Religious zeal, like religious movements, nowhere in the world causes one-tenth the stir set up by slight seismic movements in economic, political or military affairs. We still know what we live by and it is still **faith,** but it is faith in the ultimate decency of the human race and in our ability to preserve it through effective social structures.

One further statement from Fingesten:

The mature paintings of Kandinsky, Mondrian or Pollock remind one of nothing ever seen in this world. (p. 5)

This could be said with equal relevance of some designs and paintings of ancient times. Angels, dragons and devils obviously do remind us of things of this world, but calligraphy, geometry and architecture long ago got away from forms generally found in nature. Parts were recombined to form new and original wholes. More recently, the microscope and the telescope have revealed forms and designs of such infinite variety as to make one cautious about ruling anything out of nature's creations. But we need not look through a glass to observe that absolutely everything in the works of these artists—and much more besides—is indeed found in nature. Some of it, like Mondrian's, is structured and serene, but more of it is fractured, disjointed or disorganized. Diseases, wounds and breakages regularly afford examples without limit. To observe this phenomenon we simply go from the orderly to the disorderly, from the systematic to the single event or portrayal. We do this best by shutting off our senses. In a dream, trance or hypnagogic state, all the phantasmagoria of which the human mind is capable runs fast before our interior vision—dots, dashes, lines, figures, blots, splotches, colors and blank spaces. In that world everything exists; it can, under the right circumstances, be transmuted into some form of art.

There, I believe, lies the power of nonobjective art to intrigue us, move us, and perhaps inspire us. It is, to be sure, a freeing of the mind, just as reverie is, but with a difference. Nobody cares much about our personal images, dreams and nightmares, unless in their telling we become artists. Whatever else it may be, art is a form of communication, at times so complex as to require a full use of sound, sight and movement. The artist cares about **his** inner life; he strives, as it were, to bring it forth. If he is successful —needless to say, his chances are not very good— the result is a poem, a novel, a play, a painting, a sculpture, a musical composition, a dance form—a design of some kind—that arouses others and endures. His vision becomes yours and mine for the good reason that he has found in his inner thought something that tunes in with the thought of others. He has got to the mind and heart of the matter and he has done more; he has developed or perfected a medium of expression.

In a culture pattern that, for short, may be called
Western, it is permissible to ask questions without
giving answers. In fact, it is held that an answer may
be only an option or a hypothesis. As a layman, I
should like to ask one now. Eschewing faith in the
rites, rituals and mystic forms of religions, pagan or
otherwise, what may the artist fruitfully turn to? What
is truly significant as a measure of man's fate, of his
progress or deterioration as the case may be? To
me the most attractive option lies in some form of
humanism. After all, the aesthetic representations of
gods and heroes derived their power from the beauty
of the object as portrayed, reinforced by the putative
deeds of the living person. Their virtues, like their
vices, were all too human. It can be said of saints:
they were and are **people.**

Except by a curious, irrational ambivalence, science and superstition—not science and religion—are
irreconcilable. In this field of combat science has
won every battle and will continue to do so. But
science is not justice, brotherhood or love; it is not
art. Just as we cannot today embrace any form of
humanity that fails to take account of science, so
we cannot define humanity without the dominant ingredient of art. But that is simply an option which I
happen to choose, and there are others.

Suppose we choose the option of humanism, plac-
ing man at the center of his world—and humbly so,
in view of what we know about biology, geology and
astronomy. Then what may be said to be, not the
responsibility of the contemporary artist, for he has

none in this respect but the opportunity? I have a few suggestions to offer, negative and positive.

On the negative side:

Not incessant wailing; it goes against the grain of the Western world. From the beginning it has been a source of weakness in the Christian ethic. If there is to be a final whimper, the bang will come first.

No further refinement of religious symbols. Of course, for many persons their contemporary aesthetic treatment is superior to earlier forms. Still, if the inner faith is weak or nonexistent, the work, however sophisticated, is empty. Painters should paint what they see and believe, not what they ought to see or what other persons see.

No concepts, visions or rituals imported from other culture patterns wholesale unless they have displaced all else and are overmastering. The **influence** of the masters in other times or places is another matter. Artists learn by studying such works but not by any process of imitation or easy adaptation. It is all right to paint like a Theosophist or Zen Buddhist if you really are one; in fact, how can you help doing so?

On the positive side, if we hold to humanism or ethical culture, there are rich opportunities for new directions in art. For example:

The essence of modern man is, at once, to take thought and to take action. If he contemplates a navel, most likely it is not his own. A population that has to be bludgeoned into a tiny amount of physical exercise for its own sake is not likely to go far in

Yogi; nor will it, on the other hand, substitute mental emptiness for recuperative diversion. The variable states of man in which he endeavors, confronts, and encounters run the whole gamut from brutality to nobility, and these struggles are significant, come peace or war.

To some artists the post-Freudian studies of personality are still a closed book. As never before, artists could learn to react intuitively and aesthetically to the fascinating world of the mind at work or at play, and to the mind at odds with itself.

The ways in which, through the insight gained by education, each person may come to terms with danger, defeat, inferiority and mortality comprise a rich ore. It seems to me, however, that it is being more effectively worked out in the literary and performing arts on the American scene than in the strictly visual arts. To be obscure is not to be brave. The graphic and plastic arts of recent years seem obscure to many an observer. Not so modern writing and performing. It is in touch; it counts. It is not thereby necessarily cheapened. Again, speaking as a layman, I find the greatest impact or strength—I do not speak of merit—in architecture and in the design of useful objects in wood, stone and metal.

Art, in no way compromising itself, can become a powerful ally in the struggle against poverty, injustice and the brutalization of life. It can become a force for the survival of the human race, showing what is fleeting or trivial and what is precious.

Finally, it should be reaffirmed that the individual

artist need not do anything at all except to practice his art. He is not asked to save anything or anybody, including himself. He can enjoy himself. He can encourage others to enjoy themselves through the wit and humor of his creations. Personally, I wonder why so much laughter has been removed from the graphic and plastic arts. Dramatists give a high place to comedy and the great ones make of it a great art. Not being in the time of Shakespeare or Molière, we still respond to their art, whether it be in tragedy or comedy; over and over they evoke a response in depth. Surely it would be good to have some of this in every aesthetic medium.

The alternative to art as a measure of man is, I suppose, to retreat into a kind of minor league. Ortega y Gasset stated it this way **(The De-Humanization of Art,** Doubleday & Co., Garden City, New York, 1952):

Art which—like science and politics—used to be very near the axis of enthusiasm, that backbone of our person, has moved toward the outer rings. It has lost none of its attributes, but it has become a minor issue. The trend toward pure art betrays not arrogance, as is often thought, but modesty. Art that has rid itself of human pathos is a thing without consequence—just art with no other pretenses. (p. 48)

But the paradox is that, stripped of all pretenses, art retains its power as the most original and delightful of all human endeavors that get beyond the acts and events of the day. It survives all its phases. It has no place to go except forward. Man himself can do no better.

Art as Education
irwin edman

One of the advantages of being a publicly labeled philosopher is that one is licensed to speak one's mind on any subject whatever under the guise of general principles. After all, the philosopher is supposed to think about the whole universe and the whole universe includes everything in it. If the alleged philosopher happens not to know the details of what he is talking about, he is, presumably, excused on the grounds that his business is with the grand general principles and not with the sordid incidental facts. In essence, he is an authority on everything, an easy eminence which absolves him from knowing in detail, speaking with authoritative accuracy on anything. The philosopher is **ex officio** omniscient.

These cynical-sounding prefatory observations are by way of apology for my addressing a group of technical experts in the teaching of art. In one sense I have no claim whatever to address you with any rational hope of your intellectual deference or respectful attention. I have only two grounds, and they are modest ones, for addressing you at all. My own special professional interest in philosophy is in what is called aesthetics or the philosophy of art or the philosophy of criticism. I have, secondly, what does not always go with an interest in aesthetics—a strong and long-standing interest in the arts themselves. But, with respect to the arts, I am, in Santayana's

language, "an ignorant man, almost a poet, and I
am only spreading a feast of what everybody knows."
Yet, if I am to be candid, I must admit that a professional philosopher has a slight intellectual claim
to consider these matters of art with you. For the
fact is, the art teacher is an educator, not simply a
private and isolated connoisseur and technician in
the arts. Even as an educator his business is not that
of training the technical expert; his concern is that
of teaching the elements of artistic practice and
aesthetic appreciation to pupils who are human
beings and citizens and not simply irresponsible vir-
tuosi or even more irresponsible dilettanti. The art
teacher, no less than the philosopher of art, is concerned with what art is and what art does in the
wider context of general human experience. The
teacher, like the philosopher, is interested in art as
education, in much the same way that a professor of
philosophy is ultimately interested in philosophy as
an educational discipline and catalytic.

The phrase "art as education," loosely used, may
sound like mere rhetorical piety, but I am using the
term deliberately and seriously. I am submitting the
hypothesis that art, or the arts, adequately taught,
are perhaps in our day the most central and important means of education. Far too long, in American civilization, the arts have been regarded as by-
products, luxuries, isolations and escapes. Far too
long in the Western world education has been identified with the processes of the discursive, argumenta-
tive, measuring and mathematical mind. As a result,
in America the arts have been regarded as pretty

play-things, brief "truancies from rational practice," divertissement, playful exercises like lace-making or embroidery, or, in the minds of robust philistines, like cutting out paper dolls. It is a striking fact that until very recently colleges that called themselves liberal arts colleges placed almost no emphasis upon and sometimes provided not at all for education in music and the plastic arts. There has been a taint of the genteel tradition even about the study of literature.

Yet as every teacher, practitioner and historian of the arts knows, the arts have never been isolated and private. Historically and psychologically, they are part of all the wide and complicated interrelations of human experience. As Malraux points out in his **Psychology of Art,** the museum, a relatively recent invention of Western civilization, has given us a view of art objects in which we tend to think of Greek vases as having been made for display in museums and of altar pieces as having been made to be star exhibits at the far climactic end of a gallery. Meanwhile, the romantic notion of the artist, largely a nineteenth-century invention, has made the artist seem a bohemian or an irresponsible playboy. Re-education is required to make people realize that the arts are fulfillments of experience and disciplines in it and not escapes from it.

The reason that education and art have been regarded as separate matters is that there has been since the beginning of modern science an almost superstitious exaltation of the laboratory method. Mathematical analysis, language of logic and the

procedure of the technician have been supposed to
be the avenues to truth and reality. It was only
recently, and due largely to the psychologists and
anthropologists, that the importance of symbol and
form came to be seriously regarded and that the
place of imagination in education has been as adequately recognized as that of reason. I say "recently," meaning by that "recently in modern times."
But one would have to go back as far as Plato to
discover the fountainhead of art as education. Many
will recall that it was Plato who thought so seriously
of the importance of the arts as education that he
was careful both to develop a theory of what was
properly educative in music and painting and literature and what was improper and censurable. No
authority bothers to censure anything that he does
not inwardly conceive as powerful for corruption or
for edification. Plato, considering the education of
the philosopher-king and, for that matter, of the
soldier-guardian of the state also, is aware through-
out the dialogues that character is determined far
more by images than by ideas, that images come
early and come decisively, and that the soul takes
on the color and forms of those colors and forms to
which it is exposed. The temper and rhythm of
character are affected by the temper and rhythm of
the music to which one is habituated. Since it was
austere order in the soul that Plato wanted, he pre-
scribed that kind of music, that kind of literature,
which would promote the austere and stable virtues.
And he mistrusted painting altogether because it was
the shadow of a shadow of reality.

We have become suspicious of any kind of censorship, including especially the censorship of art and literature. Plato's severities are a function of his sensibilities as a poet and a teacher. No one, when he wishes to be, is a more able dialectician than Plato's Socrates. But Socrates was a wise man as well as a logician, and he knew, as we in the modern period have forgotten to know, that the shape of our world is determined by the shape of our imagination and that our imagination is shaped by the arts. He knew it because he himself so clearly gives evidence of a temperament to whom a cadence, a color, an image could mean as much as an argument.

If art is educational, in what sense does art teach and what does it teach? In the literal sense, it does not teach at all. Where it explicitly tries to do that, it is likely to fall flat in its literal mindedness. The artist who tries explicitly to teach a prose lesson, or to attach a moral to a fable, succeeds in being neither an artist nor a teacher. Art teaches not by argument or demonstration but by presentation and disclosure. It shows rather than explains; it points and points out rather than argues and proves. And what does it point up, show or disclose? In the first place, it is an instrument or vivid reminder of the sensuous qualities which our senses make available to us in the world. It obliquely and indirectly teaches us to remember what in our habituation to formality and logic we have forgotten, that there are sounds to hear, colors to see, words to be moved by. Art is, in the first instance and predominantly, an education in and of the senses.

But art educates something more than the senses. It educates the sense of form. Painting, I suspect, like absolute music, is an initiation into the values of form. The arts show in the literal sense of showing forth or presenting possibilities of form in our experience, and generate a love for order, clarity and coherence, not as a cold, intellectual assent, but as a warm and intimate realization. Nearly everyone remembers Turner's reply to a lady who was looking at one of his paintings. That anonymous dowager said impatiently to the painter, "Mr. Turner, I never saw a sunset like that." Mr. Turner replied, "Don't you wish you could?" The teaching of art is the teaching to the inexperienced in the several arts the habits of attention, discrimination and exactitude by which the perception of forms becomes both second nature and first-rate delight. It is the art teacher's business to help the student to help himself to experience form of ordered vision which the plastic arts provide. Form itself will come to be a moral criterion for him and a primary value. The arts will become anagrams of what life at its best can be: vitality fused with order and clarity made intense.

The word intense suggests a further way in which the arts operate as educators. Even those not highbrow or intellectual are living in an age of abstract formality and abstract statistical relations. Even the least statistical-minded come to think of themselves as neutral units in a society of neutral units. Between formulas on the one hand and gadgets on the other, existence becomes dull and deadened. The arts are, in addition to the education of the senses and sense of form, the education of our emotions. It is not that emotion has vanished from modern life. The shocking statistics of the prevalence of mental and nervous diseases shows how much turbulence of feeling there is in the present-day heart and how confused emotions become. The arts are a kind of therapy and, at one and the same time, a kind of fulfillment. They are also an escape in a world marked by public and private regimentation and chaos. It is therapeutic to come upon works of art which can, as Aristotle thought tragedy should do, absorb and clarify inevitable emotions. Art is an escape, not in the usual ivory tower sense, but in the subtler sense of being a liberation from regimentation, externalities, and rigidity (which always overlie confusion) to the warm pleasures of vivid form. Art is an education in fulfillment because it indicates how, within the major arts at least, frustration is not the law of the universe. Coherence can be achieved and clarity consummated. A work of art is, thus, to adopt a phrase of Santayana, nature's pledge of a possible conformity between the soul and the good.

This is, I think, what is meant by saying that the arts give meaning to life that to many contemporaries seems to have lost meaning. It is hard on a secular and scientific level to demonstrate meaning in the universe. It is difficult in a civilization bent, as our own seems to be, on suicide, to find any meaning such as that of progress to eventual good. It is hard in individual lives torn by inner guilt, emptiness and triviality to say that life has a meaning. But the meaning of a work of art does not have to be proved. It has but to be enjoyed. Here is a little world, this poem, this sonata, this statue, that makes clear and immediate sense, even if the great world, the macrocosm, does not.

What has just been said applies to all the arts, but it applies with peculiar force to the visual arts. Alfred North Whitehead, the mathematician turned philosopher, made clear at some length in **Science and the Modern World** the degree to which the minds of men in the last three centuries have been dominated by the geometric view of the world, how the formulas of mathematical physics have been presumed to be of a structure of reality. The minds of men have been hypnotized by geometry while the imagination of men has been left empty and frustrated. For the fact is that what men have felt to be real has not seemed to have had adequate expression. The visible shapes and colors of existence have been dissolved into mathematical relations; the acute intimacies of fear and hope, of happiness and misery in confrontation of the soul with the world have been explained or explained away in terms of a physical mathematical explanation of the nature of things. Time and a sense of proportion in this lecture make it impossible to give even a summary of the romantic revolt against the rationalism imposed or supposed to be imposed by modern science. Everyone knows, or at least knows about, the whole desperate flight early in the nineteenth century to vivacity or glow in the paintings of Delacroix. Poets, "simple, sensuous and passionate," to borrow Wordsworth's famous formula, whatever extremes of rhetoric romantic critics may have indulged in, were clearly on the right track, on the track at least of those aspects of experience which scientific formulas necessarily exclude and which the language of science inevitably ignores. The visual arts are a reinstatement of the senses and the emotions as avenues to the actuality of experience. Whatever refinements and abstractions are made in the realms of ideas, these refinements and abstractions have an ultimate reference to the senses. Painting and sculpture reinstate the innocence and priority of the eye. Whatever clarity logic brings to experience, there are clarities equally cogent in images impressively immediate; these are the lucidities of form, the consistencies of pattern, the coherence of style. There are forms apprehensible by the eye which are as convincing and more immediately persuasive than the formulas of discursive analysis and logical language. Even the language itself, the form of a poem, has a persuasiveness as complete as that of any formal geometric demonstration. Moreover, the visual arts convey meaning in a fashion which our rational tradition assumes is possible only in the dialectic of words. There has been a long-standing argument between devotees of abstract and representational painting, but the controversy is really an artificial one. Education in painting is discipline toward the discovery that the subject matter of a painting has meaning in terms of specifically pictorial values. The face of the young Florentine aristocrat by Barozzio is effective humanly and imaginatively moving precisely because the quality of human distinction is fused with the aesthetic distinction of the plastic means by which it is conveyed. In painting pictorial meaning and human meaning are merged; the subject matter is one with its glowing and patterned rendering. What is indicated is seen, what is felt is perceived.

It sounds like a more modest claim than it actually is to say that education in art is education in using our eyes. The claim is really a rather grand but also a genuinely justified one. For what, in fact, is being said is that to discover pictorial values is to discover much more than pictures, is to discover or to rediscover a mode of expression which gives forms significance and which, through giving familiar human objects and human situations form, renders them more alive and whole.

The world of contemporary experience is largely dominated by the formalism of ideas and the rigidities of a highly complicated and centralized society. Despite all this apparatus of organization the contemporary heart is left with a sense of emptiness and chaos. On the one hand, there is too much rigidity; on the other hand, too much confusion. It is no wonder that art is frequently called an escape, for there is a natural and plausible tendency to turn from regimentation in the outer world and chaos in the heart to the world of art, as in the art of painting, where experience for the time being becomes or remains as one chooses—for the time being, at once glowing and composed, at once radiant and coherent. The discipline in aesthetic perception may be no more than a training in response to this glow and in discrimination of this pattern. But aesthetic education is incomplete if it neglects to make clear the continuity between the world which challenges the artist to evocation of color and the achieving of order. A step in art as education is the intimation that the art of painting, like the other arts, is a projection of that ordered vitality, that equilibrium of energies which life suggests and, in a master's hand, achieves. Painting becomes a visible intimation of what is really a moral ideal, a harmony of intensities and a composition of delights.

It may seem to follow from all this I am suggesting to teachers of art that what they really are is teachers of morals and philosophy as well. In one sense this is a legitimate inference from what I have been saying. But the teaching is done not primarily by drawing explicitly the morals I have drawn but rather by making these morals patent and visible by gradually and persuasively leading students to discover in the visual arts and, by the same token, in all the arts, those values achieved by the fusion of medium and meaning which the artist makes available not by argument but by image. Those values seen in exquisite focus in works of art are the values toward which life and society ideally move. Thus, it turns out that to learn to see with steadiness and immediacy the qualities of intensities and unity in a work of art is to learn at the same time to see these qualities as the possibilities of experience in society and in ourselves. Even in a society that manages unhappily to combine regimentation and disorder, the arts suggest to the enraptured senses and the surrendered heart what possibilities there are in patterns that are free and in intensities that find their native and ordered realization. One cannot over-emphasize the liberation and challenge of such values in our contemporary world that seems on the verge of destroying these values along with everything else. The teacher of art is inevitably a teacher of possible fulfillments of experience, and the best teacher of art is, of course, the artist himself. It is he who conveys the lesson of fulfilled life in images of delight. And the values he presents are not the themes of argument but the images of enjoyment; the substance of the picture in the frame, the sculpture on the pedestal is one with what is shown as color or line.

No reflection on anything these days can responsibly be made without consideration of its consequences for the perils and contingencies of democratic civilization in the Western world. The teacher of art, the artist himself, is a failure if he deliberately teaches a doctrine, even a generous one, and a dogma however just. But is not the teacher of art, like the artist whose emissary he is, in a profound sense an educator of and in democracy? The creation of art is the self-discipline of free minds. Its order is that of individuals at once vital and self-harmonized. In art are instances, more winning than argument, of what free society may achieve.

Art: A Personal Vision
bruno bettelheim

It was my loss not to have known Charles Francis Cook in whose honor this memorial lecture is given. He was a great teacher and an art educator of rare distinction. More than that, he was a great man. Though our ways in life never crossed and my own work at present is very distant from art education, we shared one important interest: Despite his great love for the arts and his own creative talents, he seemed to have preferred working with people. It was not enough for him to introduce intelligent, well behaved youngsters to the arts at the Ethical Culture Schools. He also undertook a more difficult and challenging service to his fellow men: At the University Settlement he offered his great talents as an artist and as a man to those disturbed people who needed both of them most. In establishing the Victory Guild Psychiatric Clinic and the work camp for teenagers, to mention only these two, he combined enriching the human mind through art, with healing the disturbed mind. Though I feel strongly my own deficiencies as a dilettante in art, his example of devotion to people who need help gives me courage to speak of what we need from art in our troubled times.

Art and aesthetics, their nature and place in human life, their history—these were my first avocation. Changing interests and the vagaries of life have taken me far afield and for the last twenty years I have devoted myself to the healing of sick minds. Yet as the French like to remind us, we are always returning to our first love. I am only too aware of how far I have removed myself from what once stood at the center of my interests. At the same time, having remained an educator, I have also remained aware that creativity stands at the center of all education. So in a way, my work bridges the worlds of art and therapeutics.

Surrounded as I am every day by the incredible fertility of schizophrenic minds, I have become deeply convinced that while psychoanalysis can enlighten us about the motives and content of such originality, it tells us nothing at all about the nature of creativity or the artistic achievement. On the other hand, my daily experience with the artistic outpourings of these emotionally disturbed children was of deep interest to me for what it revealed about the delusional images that dwelt in their minds and pressed for expression—that is, for relief. And these outpourings forced me, in turn, to an important insight: That such children create images, but are not creative; that they create fantastically interesting pictures but not works of art. The most fascinating dream, expressing the deepest layers of the unconscious, is at best clinical raw material. It will not make a good poem, short story or novel. If one recalls the dream sequence that introduces Bergman's movie, **Wild Strawberries,** one realizes that in itself it is totally meaningless. At best it creates an emotional stage for the aesthetic experience to follow. It is a windup that remains an empty, misleading gesture, if no ball pitch is to follow. I am afraid that much of what we accept from students in our art classes is of this nature. Certainly all that simply expresses and fails to communicate is of this nature. Schizophrenics are not alone in their effort to create a delusional world which they cannot inhabit and where no one can join them.

To the psychoanalyst it is an appalling story how progressive education, and art teaching in particular, has responded to the insights of psychoanalysis. It is a response that shows an equal confusion both about art teaching and psychoanalysis. It is especially hard to see how art teachers came to harbor the notion that to give the unconscious free rein can be of value, either as education, aesthetics or therapy. To those interested in so-called art therapy, I might add that there is hardly a human interaction that cannot lend itself to therapeutic use: Some priests serve as therapists for troubled people, but this hardly makes religion therapeutic. Some art teachers endowed with personal skill have had a great therapeutic impact on this or that student while teaching him art; but so have some football coaches, and we do not class football as a therapeutic activity.

So much has been made of art education's freeing the emotions that I feel I should say a bit more about this idea of its therapeutic potential. It should be obvious, for example, that if artistic efforts could cure emotional disturbance, then the greater the artistic achievement, the more likely should be the cure. I need only remind you of van Gogh, whose

artistic achievement was certainly great but who, as
he reached the height of artistic achievement, first
cut off his ear, and then committed suicide. His
artistic progress neither led to a schizophrenic break
nor did it prevent one. Beethoven, as he wrote his
later compositions, perhaps the greatest master-
works of all music, was at the same time sinking
deeper into paranoia. Thus it is not the outpouring
of the unconscious, but rather the mastery of unconscious tendencies, the subjecting of creative
ability to the greatest aesthetic discipline which
alone makes for works of art. Art teachers should
know from their own creative efforts what tremendous discipline is necessary to achieve the creative
work. How then can undisciplined outpourings of the
unconscious be accepted as true creations, or as
leading to it?

Now it is true that "artistic" outpourings can be
useful for diagnostic purposes. As a matter of fact,
there are several tests in the field of visual representation that have proven vastly superior as diagnostic instruments over all more structured, more
systemized artistic efforts. They are, for example,
the Goodenough Draw-A-Man test, Rorschach's ink
blots, and Murray's TAT. All three are characterized
by mediocrity as far as aesthetic merits are concerned. The ink blots, which have no structure and
no artistic merit whatsoever, are the best of the
three, probably because they come closest to the
chaotic, wholly unstructured nature of the unconscious. I think we can all agree that the TAT pictures

have little or no artistic merit. Yet as diagnostic instruments they are far superior to the Goodenough Draw-A-Man test, though the Draw-A-Man at least gives the creative imagination a bit wider scope.

Again, what makes for creativity is not any unconscious outpouring, but the opposite: It is the outpouring rigidly worked over by a critical mind in a most disciplined way. Psychoanalytically speaking, this means the contents of the unconscious being molded and socialized by the forces of the ego and the superego. If I were to formulate my thinking here in a somewhat practical way, I would say that when the importance of the unconscious in art education was recognized, it gave art a unique role because so much of all other education is designed to repress the unconscious. But to therefore conclude that the remedy is simply to let the unconscious reign in art teaching is erroneous, is to combat the devil with the devil's grandmother. Art teaching should indeed show the student that the unconscious is not to be repressed, that it can become a source of great vitality—but only when it has been molded by the ego. What is needed is a disciplined working over of the individual and chaotic unconscious, a casting of it into forms that are meaningful to others as well as to oneself. If we achieve this for our students they will learn that an unconscious used as a natural resource can tremendously enrich the total personality, while an unconscious merely expressed leads to personality disintegration.

Perhaps a simple analogy will make the point more graphically. Freud, for good reasons, was fond of illustrating his thinking about the dynamic forces of the unconscious by drawing on parallels from the science of hydrodynamics. Sometimes he compared the mechanics of repression to a huge dam, erected to store water. Unfortunately, it is an accurate picture of much of our educational system. By erecting a huge dam of repressive measures, we dam up behind it all the instinctual pressures, and further channel into this so created reservoir added pressures from our societal demands. But by and large this educational system fails to build sluicegates into the dam. So the land below it lies fallow, remains arid, because the dam has dried up the river that used to flow through it. The result of this educational storing up and repressing is, in most cases, a dried-up personality, or an explosive spilling of water over the dam, as in delinquency, violence and alcoholism. In my example these may be likened to a breaking down of the dam, leaving destructive flood waters that drain away all its accumulated energy to no purpose.

Art educators, in this simplified example, should be aware of the power locked up in this tremendous mass of energy. If they neither dam it up nor allow it to spill wastefully over and away, they can channel and guide it to carefully laid out beds, so that the valley will blossom in a continued renewal of abundance and creation.

Much damage was done because Freud, in the interest of showing how wide was the application of his psychoanalytic insights, undertook to analyze artists and their works. But as if to warn us unconsciously that psychoanalysis has nothing to say about aesthetics, he chose for his first full-length study of an artistic creation an extremely mediocre novel. This was Jensen's **Gradiva,** which I hope none of you will ever read, because it would be a total waste of your time. But even in his famous study of Leonardo, which as Meyer Shapiro points out, is based on erroneous translations and unjustified extrapolations, Freud had to conclude that while his analysis tells us something about Leonardo the man, it fails entirely to explain why he was a great artist. And the same is true for all psychoanalytic studies of great artists. Thousands of people with the same life history and the same emotional disturbance roam the earth and create nothing, or at best empty scribbling. Again and again Freud stated that he had no answer to why certain psychological constellations that he deduced to exist in some great artists enabled them to create works of art. Psychoanalysis simply cannot explain creativity.

What happened in the wake of the warm adoption of psychoanalysis by art education is best expressed by Edith Kramer: "It seems as if the discovery of the role of unconscious processes and primitive instinctual drives in artistic creation has led to a lack of distinction between cause and effect, a confusion of the source of energy with its end results, based on the misunderstanding and over-simplification of psychoanalytic theory."* This has sometimes

*Edith Kramer, "Art and Emptiness: New Problems in Art Education and Art Therapy," **Bulletin of Art Therapy,** I, No. 1 (1961).

led to our accepting the primitive, unstructured,
or playful use of art materials. It has also led to our
taking regression for creativity or sublimation. But
the value of art teaching for the child, and of all
creative activity, does not lie in a freedom of expression that is often little more than regression, but
rather in the chance, through art, to integrate unconscious and preconscious material into ego-con-
trolled, creative work. This is doubly important because, as noted earlier, most of the pupil's other
classes inhibit the unconscious and preconscious
material from any access to the educational process.

Such procedures, based on mistaken notions of
psychoanalysis, have led art to change its meaning
away from the highly personalized, extremely individual experience that it is. Because in a strange
dialectic process unique to art—just because it
stands for the deepest personal statement made universal by disciplined effort—it becomes one of the
greatest forces binding people together without
lessening what is uniquely personal to them. It permits them to share with others in what all of them
consider something higher, something that lifts them
out of the everyday experience to a vision greater
than themselves. And this it does while making them
feel more than ever distinctly themselves. It is an
experience that sheds new meaning on the tribula-
tions of the daily humdrum of existence. It binds the
artist to his creation, and the person who experiences
art to the very same creation. Vicariously it binds
them in an aesthetic experience where even the

spectator participates in the creation of what is very best in man.

As opposed to other experiences that bind people together in something bigger than they are, the aesthetic experience does not ask them to forfeit anything of personal uniqueness, but leaves it enriched. It is a transpersonal experience that does not infringe on, or reduce the personal. Need I add that such a view of the creative experience has nothing to do with a view of art as the outpouring of the unconscious? Such a view perverts it into the opposite, a solipsistic experience that is meaningless to others, cannot be shared by them and prevents all access to any suprapersonal meaning.

In calling art "A Personal Vision" I may seem to have chosen an ambiguous title. What I meant to suggest was that all I can give you is one man's opinion about the place of art in education and the life of human beings. But I also wanted to indicate what I believe art's unique place to be: that of guiding the individual to a personal vision of the world, and of his place in it.

Contrary to theories held by some enemies of art, such as Plato and his followers, art is not an imitation of reality, neither of external reality nor the inner reality of the unconscious. It is always a vision, an attempt to express visibly what a particular age, a particular society, a particular person has viewed as the true nature and essence of reality, both the essence of man and of his relations to significant aspects of the world.

If we fulfill our calling as art educators, if we make available to future generations the chance to create order out of the chaos of their unconscious, to create a visual image of the hidden aspirations of man—as we are told the Lord created order out of the Chaos—then perhaps man will be able to shape reality in the image of his inner artistic vision.

And this has happened in history. Human progress was achieved when reality began to imitate art. Greek man in his inner attitude to life and himself tried to emulate what the sculptors had created out of their vision of what man ought to be. The Renaissance and Reformation, above and beyond the religious struggle, represented a parallel effort. Each tried to free man from being beholden to a world of the beyond. They tried to show him a vision of a world of the here and now, and of how to live in it with dignity; a vision we have still to fully translate in reality. The artists of the Renaissance and Reformation, much more than the philosophers, helped man to throw off the burden of original sin, to free himself of his sense of guilt and eternal inadequacy. Man, forming his reality in the image of the artist's visions, slow step by slow step came to feel himself a son of this earth, came to feel that this was a good world to live in, a world that was not to be negated but enjoyed in its fullness.

Similarly, Dutch genre painting was by no means chiefly a realistic image of a fragment of external reality. We are badly mistaken when we consider such paintings "realistic" because they seem that to us. For we view them from the distance of centuries in which we have been living in a world that was created in the image of the paintings. At the time of their creation such paintings were only in the most incidental sense re-creations of external reality. Actually they were conceived out of a vision of a new and better world. They are statements of defiance against a religious teaching that looked upon this world as a sham, without merit. Far from being "realistic" or imitative, these paintings are a happy vision of this world, as opposed to the next. They present to us a vision of the sanctity, the beauty, the vitality of the material world, a vision of how good life can and should be for man here and now. Their vision was in stark opposition to the official notion of our world as a vale of tears, one to be quit the sooner the better for a life of asceticism, or preferably for Heaven, which passed as the real world.*

That we have come to see this as realism in art, to see as mere representation what was actually a statement of revolutionary daring, of a new vision of the world, of a call to re-examine every known reigning value—this shows how successful these artists were in their guidance. For what followed was a radical transformation of man's inner attitude toward life. Eventually this transformation led to the rise of the natural sciences, as the scientist began to study nature as carefully in his way, as the painter had devoted minute attention to every detail of it

*Similar ideas were expressed by Erich Neumann, in **Art and the Creative Unconscious** (New York: Pantheon Books, 1959).

before him. While the Renaissance rediscovered the dignity of man by creating him in somewhat idealistic image, it was the painting of the Reformation that discovered him as an individual not in passage to Heaven, but firmly rooted in this time and this place. And with it, in a way, this gave us a vision of the future social sciences. Paintings by Breugel, for example, are also statements of the relation of man to man and to nature; no longer are they statements of his relations to God or of an ideal man.

This, then, in my opinion is the calling of art: to create for each period a vision of higher things to come. If the art educator can convey to his students the excitement such a vision confers, the student, in turn, should find it easier to commit himself to a view of human uniqueness that would inure him to the narrowness and unfreedom of a mass society. It should also protect them from being seduced, as some of the best students are, into seeking personal salvation by escaping from twentieth-century society, whether in the pretended rural settings of exurbia or in the inner retreat of the esoteric circle. Instead he will be able to set his inner artistic vision of a transpersonal meaning against the blinders of self-advancement to which the rest of his educational experience seems to guide him. Through such a vision this world of mass living might be changed, while there is still time, into a human society where people work successfully together to translate the unique personal vision into a social setting in which autonomous living prevails.

The visions of the great artists have, each in his own time and his own society, transcended his own person and place, leading his fellow men or the next generations out of their confinements toward the not yet existent, not yet realized age and society. For it is this struggle alone that dignifies our existence on earth. Artists express it through painting and sculptures. I lack the gift of translating their visions into words. Fortunately, the poets do paint with words, and I would like to quote one of them on his vision of beauty, of its nature and place in our world.

Rilke, in one of his comments on the **Duino Elegies,** separates art from therapy or social engineering, for example, saying: "Art cannot be helpful through our trying to keep and especially concerning ourselves with the distresses of others, but in so far as we bear our own distresses more passionately, give, now and then, a perhaps clearer meaning to endurance, and develop for ourselves the means of expressing the suffering within us and its conquest more precisely and clearly than is possible to those who have to apply their powers to something else." And as if he had foreseen where we should find ourselves standing today, he also wrote: "Only through one of the greatest and innermost renovations it has ever gone through will the world be able to save and maintain itself." As for the artist's task in this our world, it was: "To prepare in men's hearts the way for those gentle, mysterious, trembling transformations, from which alone the understandings and harmonies of a serener future will proceed." And here in essence is Rilke's vision, from the first of the

Duino Elegies:

For Beauty's nothing
but beginning of Terror we're still just able to bear,
and why we adore it so is because it serenely
disdains to destroy us.

Beauty, he knew, takes us to the very brink of our
existence, forces on us the harsh knowing of limitations, but at the same time opens up visions of a
world where we shall transcend our limitations and
win out over terror.

This is an experience that only a few of the greatest artists are able to make universal through form.
But it can be shared by many, perhaps all of us, if
we are taught to keep ourselves open. Only very
few in each generation can articulate this highest
vision and give it artistic reality, give it objective
existence in their work. But it can be re-created in
the human experience of many.

In this sense, great art is a learning experience.
To the art teacher falls the glory of educating his
students to be able to re-bear in themselves as a
subjective human experience what the artist has
given life to in objective form. With this as a point
of departure, I would like to mention at least in pass-
ing one further misconception about the role of art
in life that is rampant at present. It is one that cannot help having a negative influence on the education of the art educator, because his views of contemporary life and the role of art in society are
shaped by them.

To quote the Secretary of Labor: "In a complex, modern society like our own art of all kinds is called to one of the essential services of freedom —to free man from the mass. Art—whether on the stage, in a gallery, or in a concert hall—asserts the supremacy of the individual. The insight of the artist leads to a cultural discovery for all of the people."* If he is right, and I believe he is, that the great significance art can have in our own time and society is to free man from the mass, then we must beware of what would make art merely one more aspect of mass living, instead of a safeguard against it.

The number of people who paint means very little compared to what they paint and how they paint it. Yet all too often I find the correct notion—that the insight of the artist leads to a cultural discovery for all of the people—perverted to mean that all people can, by their dabbling in paint, transform their insights into art. The slogan that everybody can paint, which everybody certainly can, must never be taken to mean that everybody is an artist. The conviction that art has something of great import to say to everybody who is ready to hear it is often taken to mean that everybody who has learned to dip his brush into paint has something of importance to add to man's understanding of himself and the world.

An example from the field of music may illustrate what I mean: Hundreds of thousands of people can only fumblingly play a piece by Bach on the piano. But because of these fumbling efforts they achieve

*Arthur J. Goldberg, "To Come to the Aid of the Arts," **New York Times Magazine** (March 11, 1962).

a far greater understanding of Bach and his achievement than they would had they never struggled to re-create his music on their own. Apart from the very few great musicians, and a few others who may delude themselves into believing they are great musicians, the overwhelming majority know perfectly well that they are no artists, that while what they try to play is theoretically great music, the sounds they produce are a far cry from great, or from being creative. But they also realize that their own efforts, non-creative and non-artistic as they are, provide them with a deeper appreciation of the great artist, and a heightened trust in their own aesthetic experience of the great work of art, although it is poorly echoed in their efforts at the piano.

To continue with the example of music: In learning music a student is often asked to write some music, let's say a chorale. He usually is able to write a perfectly correct musical score. But his score almost always is so unmusical that it teaches him an unforgettable lesson in what good music is really all about, and that his own effort reveals, rather than bridges, the abyss between what he can do and what Bach achieved.

Applying this to painting, the fumbling efforts of the student are perfectly legitimate exercises, as scales are in music, and in some cases are of great value if they lead him to a better understanding of great art. But they can do this only if they are correctly viewed by the student as exercises showing him the tremendous gap between creative art and non-creative exercises in the same medium. So while his own painting is a harmless and enjoyable pass-time, and may offer him access to a better apprecia-tion of great art, with very rare exceptions it is neither art nor creative.

Therefore art educators will have to make up their minds whether painting as a leisure-time activity for the masses is a price worth paying if it reduces art to a diversion from humdrum mass living. I fear that art cannot be both: A leisure-time activity for the masses that is yet given serious acceptance, and the realization in form, the embodiment of what in a religious age might have been called the divine spirit.

Related to this and perhaps more important: I find that art educators, in writing for their colleagues, make fervent assertions of how practical art is, that it is rational and, to give it an up-to-date note, that it contributes to survival. Nor is the survival they talk of the one the pyramids assured to the pharaohs or Leonardo to Mona Lisa. If we are after practicality, rationality and survival, it would seem to me that almost any human endeavor except art had a better claim to our attention. If art can do all that, it is no longer art. We shall have to give up the notion that art can be everything to everybody, because if it is, then it adds up to being nothing of real importance to anyone.

I believe that the whole of our education has grown much too practical and rational in a narrow sense, and is far too concerned with what seems useful at the moment, as against a longer range view of life, art and humanity. I am personally in great sympathy with the humanistic tradition. This is not because of the veneration usually accorded its subject matter, often by those who have no use for it in their own lives, but because of its insistence that the educational process deal with subjects that are not necessarily practical, that do not necessarily yield monetary returns or spell success in our present-day society. My sympathy rests not with those who insist on the learning of Latin, Greek or ancient history because of the importance of these subjects. As subjects they are not preferable to many others. But my sympathy rests with those who insist on a philosophy of education that asserts that a human being must be concerned with things that don't necessarily have practical application, with matters that far transcend what might be useful at the moment, or for a particular political end. Subjects such as Latin or ancient history, when taught well, however impractical, offer wide vistas to the imagination of the human being, transcending not only the self, but also the immediate, the practical, the necessary or advantageous.

Now, I do not believe that Latin or Greek is necessarily the best way to offer future generations of Americans a chance for transpersonal, transpractical experiences. I believe that other subjects, such as the arts, can be far more effective in leading students toward a truly personal view of life and man, full of richness, imagination, comprehension, toward concerns that go beyond what is useful in the eyes of practical men.

Whatever your medium may be, or whatever the medium of your students, I believe that the main purpose of their efforts in the arts should be to convince them of the importance, first of listening carefully and trying to understand what is moving man from the inside, and then to make disciplined efforts to express it in external form, both for him to understand it better and for others to see. But even if he succeeds, that does not make him an artist. It cannot make him an artist because he is much too young for that. It takes a mature mind and a great deal of living to bear in oneself a vision of the better world for which the real artist is striving and then embodies in aesthetic form. Students can barely be taken to the threshold of a new freedom of life and experience. The task of your student, at his age, is to try to bring order and comprehension to the chaos that reigns within him. In all his other classes he is asked to deny this chaos, to repress it, to consider it invalid and unimportant. Only in your teaching can you show him that from a child, expected to take in and learn what others tell him to, he can grow into a free person struggling with and expressing his vision of himself and of life.

Here, again, the paths of the psychoanalyst and the art educator cross. Like true philosophers and healers of the mind, art educators must be good midwives, ones who try to bring into being the personal visions that have not yet seen the light of the world. For an infinitely small number your midwifery will bring into being a great or perhaps only a middling great artist. For the overwhelming majority of your students your midwifery may well be the only chance they encounter in their lives to come close to the visions of the great artists. That chance is enough for most of us, and will have to be enough for most of them.

But this is no easy task because of the institutional framework within which most of you must work. So here I would like to say a bit about the great handicap that art education has to fight against because of the inimical setting in which its teaching must operate. Our educational system per se exposes the art educator to heavy stresses because it is basically contrary to the needs of the developing individual who is seeking to realize himself. Official well-meant statements to the contrary, art teaching still has to proceed within a basically closed system. Within it our children and adolescents continue to be the victims of a cultural heritage of domination and bias, of fears and anxieties held by parents and teachers. For despite loud assertions to the contrary, these adults remain afraid of permitting children to think and act for themselves. The outcome of such domination is familiar to all of us. On the one hand we find a lack of motivation or revolt, and on the other hand an empty conformity, submission or, in fact, atrophy.

While most curricula are possibly adequate to teach biology or math or American history—though I doubt it—they give the student little chance for rising above the level of a cultural wasteland. Nearly the whole of his school experience relates uniquely and exclusively to the recorded experience of others. Most of the problems have ready-made answers in the back of the book or, more up to date, in the pre-set teaching machines. Our educational system is not concerned with originality or creativity; it is concerned mainly with acquiring a body of knowledge narrowly defined; with the memorization of facts, the finding of ready answers to problems, answers that are already known to somebody—or the test could not be scored.

Art, on the other hand, should eternally pose new problems of freedom despite our being beholden to nature and our inherent weakness. To these new problems of creative freedom each person can find his own unique solution, because no general answers are possible. I would remind you of Kant's **Critique of Judgment,** where he makes an all important point: that the essential value of the aesthetic experience resides in this uniqueness, that only about this single human experience can no true-or-false statements be made. This is the realm of imaginative freedom, where all questions, including ones about the meaning of life and of beauty, can be discussed but not solved, because their permanent solution leaves nothing to live for, spells death.

That is why I question courses that tell us how to look at pictures or what to see in them. That can only lead to teaching machines in art. Such courses are at best crutches, at worst blinders preventing an aesthetic experience. I recall how the great poets

were for decades ruined for me because I was taught
what made them great and how to enjoy and understand them. It was hard work for me later to unearth
their greatness, their tremendous personal message,
from under the rubble of teaching which had buried
them for me. But that was bad teaching. And though
we all know it, continuous watchfulness is still necessary so that a better way to create or appreciate art
can reign in our art classes.

This, then, is my thesis: The teaching of art is the
only subject in his educational experience where a
member of the future generation can be offered the
chance to truly find himself as a unique person;
because only here are there no ready-made answers
telling him what he ought to see, feel, think or in
which way he ought to find his self-realization. But
compare this with what is too often found in practice
—either the art teacher's insistence that he knows
what is good art and bad; or else the uncritical
acceptance of any outpouring as being imbued with
the artistic spirit. Neither the right-or-wrong approach
which prevails in all other subjects, nor an uncritical
acceptance of any outpourings, will give art a chance
to rectify the deadening impact on children of much
of the rest of the educational experience.

Art education, more than any other subject taught,
presents the student with the rare opportunity to
free himself at least temporarily from the falseness,
the pretensions, the trappings of our culture. But it
can only do so if those trappings are not introduced
in the art class, whether as concern with prestige,

with success in the practical sphere or with culture as a social adornment. In order to do so it must remain free of those features of the educational system that are contrary to the aesthetic experience, such as assignments, competition for grades or other expedient routines. Only then will art education leave the student open to a personal encounter with art. And by this I mean what he learns from his own inadequate efforts, and from measuring those efforts against the achievement of the great artists. This process is what gives him a chance to open the totality of his own experience to a true encounter with great art. In this meeting his own chaotic unconscious and its derivatives will be formed and aesthetically mastered both by the conscious demands of his medium and through the head-on encounter with the visions of the masters.

Here in closing I would like to refer back to my own early concern with art. Another of those early interests lay with what might be called Jewish tradition. Though an atheist, I have been deeply impressed by the poetic view of the world that some Hassidic rabbis expressed in their enigmatic sayings. Like us they were teachers, and what they were trying to teach was a religious experience freed of the shackles of institutional religion. Since art and religion have a common origin, perhaps art is destined, in our secular society, to take the place that religion once held. In any case, Rabbi Nachmann taught that: "Just as the hand held before the eyes conceals the greatest mountain, so this petty earthly life conceals from view the vast light and mysteries of which the world is full, and he who can withdraw it from his eyes, as one withdraws the hand, will behold the great light of the innermost world."

So too the constricted life of our educational system conceals from our students the vast light and mysteries of the world they inhabit. Many art education withdraw these blinders from the eyes of our students so that through your teaching they will behold the great light of their innermost world.